Redomones

and

Eye to the Future

Poems by
Alan MacGillivray

K&B
Kennedy & Boyd

To the Memory of
Robert Bontine Cunninghame Graham
(1852-1936)
Scottish writer, traveller, politician,
Socialist and patriot.

"Una tierra sin caballos, un pueblo sin sueños"
(A land without horses, a people without dreams)

Contents

The Broch of Glass

Hildina in the broch of glass
Waits for the southern wind
To bring the ships of the Orkney Jarl
To where she is confined.

By day she stands on the highest wall
Looking beyond the tides,
By night her lantern dimly gleams
Through the tower's glassy sides.

At Yule she huddles her feathery cloak
Fast round her body's chill,
In voar she walks o'er the springing grass
Where the broch's stones meet the hill.

Through simmer dim her white skin glints
More bright than the broch's glass walls,
But the golden hairst brings no remead
To Hildina's anguished calls.

In the morning the sea is still and bare,
Her lover sends no release,
The afternoon brings not the hope
That her loveless years may cease.

In his cave below the bird-filled cliff
The Solan Laird sits tight.
Hildina must come at last to him
One merry-dancing night.

(Broch: an ancient tower built for defence near the sea; Solan: gannet)

In Balladia

I

Out of the black nor'east, when all hope had almost gone,
See, says Lady Maisie, waving her empty glass, *a ship*.
Surely, yes it was, back from Norroway. The bold Sir Patrick
Himself, crew dog-tired, vessel storm-battered, wrapped around
With finest silks and golden twine, saved from wrack.
Riding that old Dunfermline road, who to meet him but the eldern knight.
Welcome back, dear Spens, such feats of seamanship!
I'll sort you, pal, Sir Patrick grits, *can't get rid of me.*
King already hammering the vino, *Great to see you, Pat,*
Have a snifter, slowly subsiding in hiccups,
Hauf seas owre, under the regal table
 With the Scots lords at his feet.

II

Things were getting fraught at Ushers Well.
Maids complaining about the briny footprints
On the flagstones and the wringing sheets;
The cook miffed that her special dishes, even
The cullen skink, were being slighted; the three sons
Themselves dripping weed and crabs around, scaring
Bejasus out of dogs and horses; parlour-maid with heebies
Every time the youngest looked at her; cocks struck
Dumb without a cockadoodledoo. The old witch-wife
Beginning to find three idle zombies round the house
Not what she'd bargained for. *Out with you,* she says,
With a suitable curse. And off they have to trudge,
Over the machair, crunch on the shells, heads
Disappearing under the lazy swell, back to their place.
And then, the gathering clouds, a rising wind,
Fashes in the flood, returned, unexorcised, for ever.

III

So when her lover grows to giant size, stamping his foot,
And the ship begins to spin and sink, what else to do
But fire off a maroon into the frosty air, shrug on the yellow
Jacket, secure the strings in front with a bow, and blow
More air into the tube. Shoes off, down the slide.
Then, in the water, switch on the light, blow the whistle
And wait. *For God's sake, woman,* says the lifeboat cox
(Her husband, as it happens), *what are you playing at?*
This is the third time this year. Get a grip.

IV

There she is, five months gone, clutching Tam
While he diverts himself with metamorphosis,
Newt and adder, bear and lion,
Slippery, smooth or hairy, any shape,
You name it, while Janet sweats and spits,
Digging her nails in, squashing, stumbling,
Until, for Pete's sake, a red hot iron bar.
Well, sod this for a game of soldiers,
She thinks, and lets him drop. Off he flies,
Back to Elfland or wherever, and she sighs
With relief, catches the Fairy Queen's eye
And giggles. *No man is worth it, dear,*
Believe me, I know. Call me Maeve.
And off they go, Janet behind astride.
I know a good adoption agency, says Maeve.

V

Back home after seven years who knows where,
Crap shiny suit, green suède shoes, utter naff.
See that Elfin Queen, she was a goer, I can tell you.
No kidding. Melrose Sevens, in the refreshment tent,
Shooting a line - deserts, rivers of blood, strange
Roads, magic apples, bags of nookie, lots more.
Can you believe the man? Sold his car to a guy,
Swore it was in good nick, regularly serviced.
First time on the road in seven years,
All the electrics failed. Don't think he means
To deceive, just convinced he has the tongue of truth,
Like all bad poets.

Returning to Lanark

The War
It is still a war, of course, holy or not;
Mansoul lies yet in jeopardy
and the Metropolis of the World is under siege.
Coming by train to Greater Unthank Central,
glass-roofed and sunny with pigeons,
we keep in our pockets not loch shells and grit,
but hologrammed gay credit cards and mobiles.
Thus can the Institute track us, City Hall keep tabs,
Global-Monboddo input the latest data to our profile.
Out in the hinterlands, the no-fly zone,
the oil and drug cartels, militias, mercenaries
grunt and push around the bomb-fragmented flesh.

The Epic
Received convention is to plunge *'in medias res'*.
Begin with that sudden frantic sense of being a stranger;
this is not a world I recognise, the streets
dingy and pot-holed, put-upon and down-ground people
wearing their diseases under cheap naff clothes,
loud-swearing neds and drunks on buses,
the young betrayed to emptiness in homes and schools.
The oracle should speak to all, recount the Fall,
how when you think that it is sorted,
education, health, a kind of justice quite secured,
in creep again the posh-voiced bronzed Corinthians
to sack and burn the nanny-state,
tossing you as a bonus to the corporate wolves,
old pals, old bullies, same old same old Trojan Horse.

The Great Leviathan
See how land shakes and breaks, the coasts dissolve,
waves sweep in, the mountain slides away,
cities flood, reactors crack, the twisters swirl.
Can we no longer trust this solid earth?
We grew up planted on our Scottish rock,
knowing some things were founded fast.
We did not know that wind and rain,
so fresh upon the face, could bring
the curies to the mountain burn,
the rads to lambs, the becquerels to garden produce.

Above the warming tides of long futurity
the bright-faced culprit lurks in open view,
flaunting his winds, his flares, spots and all,
blessing us daily with his kindly light.

Recording for Eddie

That must have been a time of happiness...
With headphones on, the outer voice is muffled.
Crisp words, hard, sharp on a square of brightness,
I have read you aloud, calm, unruffled,
So often, am I doing you justice
Now, closed in a booth, no eyes to contact?
Knitting of ear, eye, voice – that's how trust is
Engendered. Will once more create impact?
"We'll go with number one." But you will notice,
 Listening through your poet's radio mast
Tuned to the finest pitch, if what you wrote is
Lacking its dynamic unsurpassed
Felicity. These thistle days show how remote is
Your wilting even in the hardest blast.

Morganstern

Jump
into the sun, he said. And so we did.
Throughout that spacious star we steered and hid
ourselves in sport among its many ways
and secret spots, that fiery teasing maze
of astral language, light that flared and wrought
out lofty naves of unintimidated thought,
and reservoirs of energetic dreams
to feed imagination's jetting streams.
Till, caught by bubbling light, intensely pinned
in cheerful eloquence of solar wind,
we burst out through the flaming photosphere
and found ourselves on course for swinging near
each planet-child of that prolific source.
The first, a place of such dear kindly force
as gave its green compact communities
a thousand couthy opportunities
to bless their folk, enabled us to know
this wind that carried us was love. And so
to a second world, a realm well starred
with hills, with glens, cloud-crossed, full-watered, hard
to traverse, know, even at times to love
entirely, were it not that, caught above
that thistly land, we saw love's light contain
it in a jewelled sonnet. On again
to further worlds: a multilingual Earth,
its satellites of wisdom, moons of mirth;
a belt of asteroids in tumbling race;
a planet with an outward gaze on space
to speculate beyond convention's bounds,
confront whatever overawes, astounds;
and, last, the great gas giant, passion's fire,
erupting, coming out in fine attire.
All breathless, overcome, we left that sun
to rule its empyrean, turned to run
quick to our lesser system. Looking back
in elegiac mood, we watched a black
advancing shadow of eclipse move slow
across the star's face, full concealment, no
mere transit this, the real deal. Was this
the way to say goodbye, blankly dismiss

all we had known? Yet just at final blink,
before the dark, a bead of light, the chink
of radiance we'd read about, a ring
effect with jewel bursting out, what bling!
We hugged each other, shared such joys.
See, on our screens. The diamond, ah boys,
the diamond!

(The "diamond ring" effect is a feature of many solar eclipses, immediately before or after the moment of full eclipse.)

Maighstir Norman

It is disconcerting, to say the least,
that a man in my position
cannot walk at ease to relish
this highland landscape of his fathers
without a lean Zen Calvinist
dominie striding before,
flicking his fags aside
and jabbing a long sardonic finger
hither and yon to pick out
this and that bird and ben,
frog and loch, stag and burn,
saying, Here is a piece of reality
and see, it is a jewel,
shaped in my language, but not to crystal,
only to its own essential self.

Plato inverted, truth drawn from shadow:
basking shark resurfaced,
    deer skeleton refleshed,
        recodified amazing mister toad.

Day on the Hill

To know that mountain, make an early start
If you want to savour what it has to give.
You'll never take in all, as long's you live.
Yet stride its natural range and know its art –

Each crag a novel, every burn a tale,
Bog-myrtle, bracken, heather, sketching clear
So many small harmonious smile- and tear-
Inducing truths – to temper History's gale

And guide the skeins of wild returning geese.
Do not omit to stoop and study flowers
Or stones, poems that concentrate the powers
Of larger works – for all is of a piece.

Come from the hill at last in evening glow,
Richer through knowledge of a real Munro.

Callanish

With the others, he stands on the skyline,
prim and dignifies, erect in stern propriety,
a Wee Free minister to the life.
By him, a cailleach with her creel
bends in centuries' submissiveness.
The rest, more indistinct, a misty
congregation of anonymous faithful,
make up the circle round their god.
Come closer, see, they are mere stones.
Religion's archetypal image, senseless
and unthinking ring of faith adoring
elevated megalithic vacancy.

Sheep in Harris

Surly old guy
firmly settled on the tarmac verge
not shifting for you
or anybody.

Two young sparks
full of testosterone
ramming horns in rivalry
ignoring swerving cars.

Desolate mother
silent by the carriageway
unable to leave her precious child
lying in blood.

Sheep, eh!

Anger
(i.m. J.T.)

Angers accumulate with passing years,
Some so strong they never go away
But sit in special rooms within the mind
To be avoided, formally revisited,
Or stumbled into on a darkling day.

I do not speak of these, but rather of that
Which follows on the loss of one, not dear to you,
Not marked by tears of your own grief
- Finding the sudden empty desk in front,
Seeing the stunned parents in the mourning pew,

Creating for those left uncomforting respite
Within the classroom's calm routines.
Is it professional anger at a talent's waste,
Frustrated vanity of Dominie Pygmalion
Losing another host for vital cultural genes?

Nothing so cold upon that sunny day
When in the sandstone street of a small Border town
I listened to his friend tell how, the hired car parked,
They went to view the Pentland Firth,
Which hunched its back and coldly licked him down,

Taking from that rock at Durness all his
Seventeen-year-old enthusiasm, quiet smile,
Amused intelligence, a proud new pass
In Higher English, no genius but a dogged wish
To shine somehow, like Sage Carlyle,

Whose birthplace he grew up beside.
I felt that moment's heat of anger soon subside,
Succeeded by this chill occasionally returning tide.

Horatian Ode

(i.m. Joseph P. (Joe) O'Neill, 1929-2008)

The rain drenched a grey Glasgow when we said
Goodbye to you, Joe, in your red church.
Your friends, who knelt or raised the cup and wafer
Or merely sat in grace,

Could not but feel your warming presence rise
To fill the space. Neither eucharist nor
Formula responses, not the singer
Nor the liturgy,

Could match that genial heat that stirred the memory –
The kindly chair of meetings, sudden laughs,
A slight acerbity, humane analysis
Of poets' passion.

Intrigued to hear about a past self, Brother
Francis, to recognise you in "Our Dad"
So praised by grown-up son and daughter,
To share the priest's "My friend".

What sound did that occasion lack for me?
Your voice in "She moved through the fair"
As you so often sang it long ago,
Setting the Irish in you free.

What more was missing? Language at its best –
Some lines of Yeats, perhaps – the tongues of child
And scholar too? I think you would have liked
To hear a word of Gaelic,

And Latin, of course, some Horace, I feel –
Integer vitae scelerisque purus
Non eget Mauris jaculis, neque arcu... .
Nothing to fear, Joe, at the end.

Remembering Jimmy
(i.m. James Inglis)

I didn't tumble to your trick
at first, merely felt disconcerted
looking at your glass eye while
the good one inspected me unnoticed.
That was at my interview, but still
thirty years later I was being caught out.

"Take a minute now to remember Jimmy
as you would wish to remember him,"
your son said at the crem the other day.

Only a minute indeed,
                    as the curtains closed.

The slightly bandy walk along the corridor,
the department meeting where yours was the only voice
and sixteen seasoned teachers held their wheesht,
the brisk and sudden rollocking succeeded
by the throaty chuckle and a one-eyed humorous glint.

Intellectual rigour grafted on to humane passion,
the constitutional authoritarian, unsentimental man of feeling,
pugnacious pacifist,
a vegetarian who'd gnaw an argument's wasteful flesh
and spit out bones of logic.
Yon's the true democratic intellect.

I have seen your video
modelling good classroom practice;
"Voltaire imparts Belles Lettres to the Gilded Airdrieonian Youth".
Small wonder your professional memorials are courses
for the unchallenged and the supernormal,
wider horizons for the later learner.....

Other things surprised me.
I did not know the grandpa who knew the names of plants,
the gardener, the concert-goer, art-lover,
brandy connoisseur, the battler for Amnesty International.
But I can believe them.

Every day at ninety-three you took Jenny out
for her breath of air. It took a cauld breath
of snowy Glasgow air to catch you
at the end.

Did Death do a double-take then,
fixing your already dead eye
with his chill gaze, before suddenly
noticing your warm human one
having the last laugh?

Big Guy on the Town

It is 11:15 in Glasgow a Saturday
the day before St Andrew's Day, yes
you've guessed this is O'Haraspeak, and
it is 2003 and I come off the 44 bus
at Central Station and I go get a Herald Tribune
in W H Smith's on the concourse
because later in the day I will sit with a certain person at home
and do the crossword despite the baseball references
which we do not know but still endure

I walk across to Borders as it starts to rain
and browse among the Scottish books to see if there
is anything new by Eddie Morgan or Donny
and the other boyos but there is nothing
and I pick up Interzone on the way out

I go over to the Woolwich
and the machine doesn't even blink at my PIN
before it sicks out a batch of crumpled Royal Bankies
and I go on up Buchanan Street
across St Vincent Street on the green man
and into the Pier to look at bronzey statuettes

and then right up the steps at the top
into the Royal Concert Hall and wait in line
for tickets to the Children's Christmas Concert
and as I come down the steps again a wee boy
says Who's thon big green guy wi the specs/

and I was standing on the stairs in Dillon's
looking at the middle-aged guy
who looked back at me over his evening paper
with the big guy's photo and the headline
DONALD DEWAR DEAD

Lord of the Dance

(i.m. James Muir)

Sunt lacrimae rerum.........
Virgil got it right, as he did so often,
To make the pious Aeneas weep
Before the images of vanquished Troy.
Yes, tears for things indeed; and all those
Passing outcomes of mortality touch the mind.
So when the music chimes with coffin's
Placement on the final dais, the blessed secular strain
Evoking images of man and wolf
In symbiotic movement on a darkening plain
Upon a silver screen, the tears surprise the eyes,
The mind is touched and we are drawn
Into the celebration of a life.

All lives are exceptional, and each one's life
Sparkles in its own exceptionality.
Thus a youth growing up in Fife and finding love;
A man discovering books and language;
A teacher passing on intangible and priceless wealth;
A husband and father fostering and focusing
A nuclear community of warmth, security and love;
And, too, a writer forming new mortal things
In verse and story – sure, there must be tears,
Brief tears of loss, but more enduring drops
Of happiness that such things have truly lived.

As in the film, where watchers on the plain
See in amazement man and animal create
A new artistic wholeness in their dance,
So we have been blessed in seeing
And being touched by this man's life,
Mortal as all things are, yet shaping in its artistry
An image of enduring things that need no tears.

Thank you, Jim. You tell us yet again,
Whatever life presents, the answer's Yes.
There is no fail, the words and works prevail.
You're right to the end, Jim, write to the end,
Right to the edge, dancing with wolves.

Esperanzas

(On the night before the burial of his wife, Gabriela, on the Isle of Inchmahome in the Lake of Menteith, Robert Cunninghame Graham dug her grave himself, assisted by one of his old tenants. On its completion, he sat in the Abbey ruins and smoked a cigarette in accordance with her wishes. Thirty years later he was laid beside her.)

I

(September, 1906)

Aye, Laird, draw breath afore the grey day's dool.
We've howked awa aa nicht by lantern glow
Tae mak yir leddy's grave. The morn we'll row
Her ower an lay her doon. In yon dunk mool
Will there be hopes as weel tae tyne an leave
Fur worms? The bairns ye niver had, the hoose
Upby ye lost, the ridin days fitloose
Tae seek lost cities, gowd tae fill yir nieve,

The richts o warking men, Scotland remade,
A horses' haven, an Guid kens whit mair.
Pit them there, these fancies, doon in the clay.
She'll haud them safe.   Sakes, Laird! Ye've shairly paid
Yir debt tae youth an hope, an ample share.
See, it's getting licht, could be a braw day.

II

(September, 1936.)

My auld grandfaither tellt me he an you
Dug oot this grave ye're lyin here aside,
Tellt me, whit's mair, you were a man could ride
These Menteith roads an parks the haill day through,
Practised lang syne ower aw thae pampas doun
In Sooth America, forbye in Spain.
It's yir advice on that I culd be haein
The noo, seein that I'm aff this eftirnune.

This Spain, ye ken, the bluidy civil war.
A thinkin fellow cannae jist staun by
While honest workers can dae nocht but dee.
I'm shair yersel wad rise an ride, an daur
The deils. Syne frae the grave I hear ye sigh,
 "The deid can open mony a livin ee."

(Los muertos abren los ojos a los que viven - inscribed on the memorial plaque to Gabriela Cunninghame Graham above her grave.)

King Robert IV

(When asked by a lady if it was true that he was the strongest claimant to the Scottish throne and might one day be King of Scotland, Robert Cunninghame Graham replied, "Yes, I believe that is true. And what a three weeks that would be!")

His brief benevolent despotic reign
Saw startling changes made throughout the land.
Blatant respectability was banned
(Except in Edinburgh); trips to Spain
And South America were added to
The school curriculum; a law was made,
Protecting discreet *demi-mondaine* trade;
All titles were abolished, any who
Maltreated horses were condemned to die,
The poor and sick received their rightful dues.
Such misrule gave offence. It came to pass,
One day he saw a guillotine dragged by
The Art Club window, knew he had to choose,
Lit out on horseback for the seas of grass,

Where, last was heard, an exiled king still moves,
Proud, noiseless, printless, upon unshod hooves.

Trapalanda

The greens and greys and blues are shining on
my wall as bright as when the painter (was
it Lavery or Creeps? I have to pause
to think) created that Edenic dawn.
The horses run in their tropillas just
as once they did on the unparcelled range,
unshod and silent round the drowsing strange
lost city of the Indios, where I must
in final days arrive, accompanied
by those I rode with in a youthful passion,
Exaltación, Raimundo, gaucho-fashion,
before these years of loss, Gartmore, dear Chid.

The picture hangs in space, it never was.
The art that should have been transcends all laws.

A Hero of the New World

After the dusty parade in the Plaza Mayor   *the main square*
by the League of Youth
and the veterans of the War
of One Hundred Days,

after old Esteban has murdered 'The Flowers of the Forest'
on his faded pipes
and folded them away
for another year,

the doctor and the chief of police
resume their unending chess game
outside the Café Tierras Altas   *the Highlands Café*
over a whisky-soda,

Angus García and Hector Chisolmo
lead their mestizo teams to battle   *mixed race*
with a pigskin ball
in the hour before the dark,

and the wind that blows without obstruction
between the Cordillera and the Southern Ocean *the Andes mountain range*
divides around the statue
of El Abuelito Escocés,   *the Scottish Grandad*

Libertador of Nueva Alba,   *Liberator*
Friend of the Caudillo,   *the Leader*
exile from his distant North.
In a different age he came,

shepherd in his calling,
scholar in his dreams,
soldier in a new land's extremity,
Gaelic, English, Spanish on his tongue.

With the mountains in his eyes,
the northern seas within his mind,
he stands in his own future, in the unceasing wind
across the horizontal grass.

Between the condor and the albatross
the golden eagle hovers still.

Las Cabras   *(The Goats)*

They have felled the pines
    in the Arroyo de Sueño   *the Gully of Dream*
where the cicadas whirred
    through the midday heat,
and the 'pisos de lujo'   *luxury flats*
    and the 'ropa de diseño'   *designer clothes*
reign where the goats
    placed their nimble feet.

In those years the Ermita   *hermitage, shrine*
    was alone on its hill
and the Virgen looked out
    down the lonely track.
Yet the faithful come
    with flowers still
past developers' flags
    and the salesmen's shack.

Above the swish
    of incessant sprinkling,
on the next hillside
    to the newest block,
you may just catch
    a melodious tinkling
as the goatherd drives
    his diminishing flock.

And perhaps there is caught
    on a dried-up thorn
a black and white twist
    of nanny-goat's wool,
or a fragment shed
    from the billy-goat's horn,
and the guests may find,
    with shocked eye-poppings,
a warm and steaming
    cluster of droppings
on the pure green grass
    by a blue-tiled pool.

Boatsang

(From "Barcarola" by Pablo Neruda, *Residencia en la tierra*, 1935.)

Oh gin ye wad but touch ma hert,
gin ye wad but pit yir lips tae ma hert,
yir dentie mou, yir teeth,
gin ye wad pit yir toung laek a reid arra
whaur ma bruckle hert is duntan,
gin ye wad blaw owre ma hert, aside the sea, greetan,
it wad dirl wi a kittlie soun, the soun o the wheels on a dwamie train,
laek shiftan watters,
leaves in hairst,
laek bluid,
wi a soun o a drowie lowe birnan the lift,
dramean laek dwams or brainches or blousters
or the mane o a dowie hythe,
gin ye wad blaw on ma hert aside the sea
laek a whitely ghaist
on the rim o the faem
in the set o the win,
laek a lowsened ghaist, on the strand o the sea, greetan.

Laek a naethin hingan on, laek a deid-bell's jowe,
the sea pents the soun o the hert
in smirr an gloaman on a lanely shore:
nicht faas wi nae misdoot
an its wracked an blae-mirk standart
stowes wi a dirdum o siller plenits.

An the hert stounds bitter laek a roaran buckie,
caas; oh sea, oh coronach, oh mizzled dreid
skailed in mishanters an brucken shouders:
the sea wytes wi its stound
its liggan scaddows, its green puppie-flooers.

Four Sonnets of Garcilaso de la Vega

I
Cuando me paro a contemplar mi estado...

When I pause to take stock of my situation,
And look back over the steps that brought me here,
I find, depending on how misguided my journey was,
I could have landed in a lot worse shit;

But when I pay no heed to the road,
I've no idea how I've landed in such a mess;
I know I reach my end, and indeed I've regretted
Seeing my cares dying with me.

I shall have succeeded in devoting myself clumsily
To Someone who'll know how to ruin and finish me
Whenever she wishes and will relish doing it;

So if my own desire can kill me off,
Hers, which isn't really on my side
And has the power, has no option in the matter.

II
En fin, a vuestras manos he venido....

Okay then, here I am at your door,
Ready to face the inevitable.
Whining about it won't do any good,
Not in the book of rules you've written for me.

Looking back, what has this experience amounted to?
Nothing more than a sustained example
Of how the sharpest cuts are given
In the action of surrender.

I see now that pouring out my feelings
On such a dry and bitter tree
Produced only bad fruit and worse luck.

What I feel now is sympathy for you
As you gain no more satisfaction from my obsession.
All you now can have is pleasure from the final kiss-off.

III

La mar en medio y tierras he dejado...

I've left behind the sea and lands in the midst
Of whatever good I timidly possessed;
Going further away every day,
I've passed peoples, customs, languages.

I'm already distrustful of going back;
I think of remedies in my imagination,
And the one that I hope is most certain is that day
When both life and care will end.

What could save me from any harm
Would be seeing you, Lady, or hoping
For the possibility of hoping without losing it.

But already not seeing you stops me from benefiting,
For if it is not death, I find no remedy,
And if it is, I still won't be able to have any.

IV

Un rata se levanta mi esperanza....

My hopes arose for a while.
But, so weary at having arisen
They fall again, reluctantly leaving
Their place free for mistrust to enter.

Who will suffer such bitter change
From good to ill? Oh, weary heart!
Accustomed after fortune to have prosperity,
It now struggles in the poverty of your state.

I myself shall undertake by force of arms
To shatter a mountain, which another might not break,
Set about very thickly with a thousand obstacles.

Not Death nor prison nor any hindrances
Can prevent me from going to see you, as I wish,
Nor any naked spirit nor man of flesh and bone.

Stone Poem

COMHRUITH
Stone, water, people
leave their trace.
Three streams joined,
folk held this place
between the hills
through change and squall.
Work as one,
share it for all.
COMRIE

Legend for Sisyphus Stone

SISYPHUS do you not see that as you strain and push eternally up against
my rough and uncomplaining mass you move toward that ultimate
condition of being beyond the now and here and when I slip from sweaty
failing grasp as was foredoomed and send you sliding stumbling down
to try again it is because you are not fit as yet to stand upon the height of
death – the necessary end which you are seeking to evade – giving you still
assurance you will reach the peak where light and distance open up before
you and you see the unexpected future and rest your hands relaxed and
gentle on the rainwashed sunwarmed welcoming STONE

Turn of the Season

Trust me, yon sad familiar ice must crack,
A changing climate will take care of that,
The frozen soil, this grey veneer, the flat
Stone-faced indifference to a people's lack
Of zest, of colour, scent, mouth-filling smack
Of triple-decker language, will take heat – and what
Bright creatures then reclaim their habitat,
Marking anew our glen's neglected track.

While you, who look to see by Andrew's croft
A crisp new birch wood springing to the broch,
Blue haze of butterflies and harebells curled
Around the well, a solan's soar and loft
And heart-arresting plunge into the loch,
Stand guarantors of our enlarging world.

Vision

They are to come, the burgh's best days yet,
The empty shops restocked, all streets alive,
Greyfriars to Midsteeple's ringing net
Of song; beyond, street theatre's pulse and drive.

Under the Dock Park trees those warmer nights
Bring out the dancing couples by a deepened Nith,
With laden barges moored beneath the lights.
Accents and colours mingle here, wherewith

A happier age, an easier world at peace,
Embrace this ancient toun, a new Dumfries.

Cockcrow

I heard a cock's crow faint
before six this morning
under the shared breathing in the bed
beyond the lined curtains
and the double-glazing
above the first traffic noise
over the bungalows and semis –

Not a sharp assertion
as in the light-drenched Sabbath air
it used to come across
the perfect hill-reflecting loch
through the blue peat-smoke
ascending straight from Stewarts' chimney
and in the tobacco-tin-wedged open skylight
to the box-bed and a drowsing boy –

Yet it is good to know
that Chanticleer still lives
hailing a new day in bourgeois land
up by the wind farm
and the pyloned moors

Dominus Reconstructus

Here I sit, the amiable alien,
teleported in from elsewhere,
come to 'inspect' Miss S.,
the student, quivering with nerves
and worksheets. I make
mysterious notes, smile at
appropriate points, bend a quizzical gaze
upon undisconcerted boys
and bold-eyed girls.

When the time is right, I rise
and 'circulate' around the
randomly-assembled groups
feigning discussion of a
non-significant question.
The whispers follow me around:
   'He's awfy tall';
     'There's flooers on his shirt';
      'Does he fancy her?'

Yet could these victims of a
post-permissive age but see behind
the rimless glasses and the smiling
eyes, soft suède loafers,
the jacket and the strides,
to glimpse the crumpled suit,
the polished shoes, that long
black gown with rips and chalkdust,
the hard suspicious weight
in either dangling sleeve
of red-edged hymnbook,
coiling leather tawse,
waiting to rear and loose
the whirlwind of a guid
Scots education
on their soft, indulged, unstretched
and unsuspecting noddles.

A Lear of the Suburbs.

"Enter Lear with Cordelia dead in his arms."

I did not choose this part.
I did not audition with the RSC.
I did not learn the words
Nor was I fitted for the kingly robes.

I did not stand before the Court of Britain
And divide my kingdom.
I did not wander the houseless moor
And rage against the gods,
Calling the winds and rain
To bring down havoc on a corrupted world.
I did not rave and weep,
A poor rejected mad old man.

I have lived my life in quiet streets
Doing the world's necessary work,
Thinking I was happy.

Why then has it come to me
At this late hour of life
To bear this unnatural load?

A Good Day for Mr Pepys

-th July, 166-.
In bed, my wife and I had merry talk.
Thence to the office where did write commission
for Captain Kirk to King's new ship "Ambition".
At Whitehall, waiting on his grace of York,
did speak with Mr Evelyn on the scheme
to mingle blood in dogs, and after dined
with several on a sturdy pie, well wined
and aled. There I found the girl did seem
aimable that I kiss her and toucher sa chose.
In the theatre, saw Nelly entertain
the King and beauteous Lady Castlemaine.
Much beer and oysters kept us till we rose
late. Then home to songs and music, prayers said,
my nightly draught was brought. And so to bed.

View from the Gallery Wall

Ah yes, I'm still here after all the years
That time has taken from you. It appears
That I have worn the better. That young man
You were has withered, as has every one
Of those who followed, standing where you are
In shabby coat or crumpled suit, the star
Of your own life, the Man without a Name
Come yet again to the Beautiful Mrs Graham,
To play your part of dumb adoring fan
Like many another weak besotted man.

It is the eyes that I remember best.
Some, like yours, are over-guarded lest
A depth of feeling should be suddenly apprised
By those around one in the throng, disguised
Through years of Scottish caution. I can read
Most other gazes well, feeding my need
To know how people see me, here arrayed,
Posed with a plume, feeling the rich brocade,
Foot poised as if to step out of the frame
Playing the role of haughty wilful dame.
There is a sort of man who'll frankly dote,
Scanning my lips and eyes, bosom and throat,

Seeming to say, "If you were mine, my girl,
You'd know it, that would really be a whirl",
But other men, as drawn to me, yet fear
That which their nature tells them, hide their leer
Under a mask of something close to hating
And move on past, found out, self-deprecating,
Resenting who I am and what I do,
Feeling that I disdain them through and through,
A false surmise. The women are more shrewd
In apprehending that the pure, the lewd,
Are equally inconsequential, as their gaze
Inspects my height and elegance, surveys
The bodice and the skirt, the hat, the hair,
The slightly sullen look of near-despair.
Here, they deduce, the statement of a life,
I the possession, I the trophy wife.

Two pairs of eyes determine my whole being.
The first I remember, Tom the artist's, seeing
My emergence at his brushes' strokes,
Staring into my soul as he invokes
The truth of her, the subject of his art,
The Honourable Mary Graham, née Cathcart,
Fair North British heiress, teenage bride,
Society beauty, Perthshire's toast and pride.
She comes to look, both gratified and shy,
Wearing that dress, and stammering, "Why,
Mr Gainsborough, this is wondrous braw!"
Her large eyes then, and later, looked in awe
Until they grew too large, and then, no more.
Tom (her husband)'s eyes I last recall
Being wet. That was before the sudden fall
Of dark about me. Where I stood and why
Within that dark I do not know. But my
Next light was here within this stately room
And here I must remain, so I presume.
In this room the people come and go
Talking of my friend, Thomas Gainsborough,
Who made me stroke by stroke and dot by dot,
Looking at Mrs Graham, whom I am not.

One thing keeps puzzling as I watch you back -
Where have they gone, why do I ever lack
The comfort of their gaze? They came and smiled
And went, they passed and glanced, and thus beguiled
Me in the boredom of my endless stance,
A silver wallflower waiting for a dance,
Tom and Tom and Mary, unreturning,
And all the others after. Are they spurning
The beautiful Mrs Graham? Do I fail
You in some way? I can never be hail-
Fellow-well-met, and yet I look, I trust,
Approachable. Will you decide you must
Go, too? Your hair is white, is that a sign?
The white-haired always go, traverse my line
Of sight for one last time, and then
Are lost.
            This must not happen. Come again!

Elegy on some Gentlemen of Fortune

You had the best of everything,
You, my brave lads, with the curls and moustache,
The elegant villain's beard
And swords with twirly hilt and flashing blade.

The best sets............ Hollywood palaces with panelled walls
In which to clasp the blonde décolletée princess,
Stone-effect castles with their flagstones
And a spiral staircase perfect for swordplay
And a drawbridge to be let down in the nick of time
For that final splendid charge that saves the day.

The best clothes......... ruffles, lace, the floppy hat,
The leather belts and shiny breastplate,
Elegantly distressed tunic,
Those (definitely masculine) tights, an oiled and hairless chest,
And, ah, the boots, the boots, soft and sexy and supple,
The swaggerer's dream.

The best names.......... Rudolf and Captain Blood,
Robin of Locksley, Guy of Gisborne, Black Michael (Prince of Sneers),
Scaramouche, d'Artagnan, Zorro with his Mark,
Rupert of Hentzau, and the Captain from Castile........
And all the names behind the names – Errol, both the Douglases,
Basil (swordsman par excellence), Tyrone, Ronald, Burt,
Still alive in monochrome and Glorious Technicolor
(By arrangement with Natalie Kalmuss).

The best lines........ hacked from a thousand scripts
Some nuggets glint: "Swell, sails, and bear us on";
"One for all and all for one"; "I cannot stand a man
Who fights with furniture"; "Rassendyll, you're the finest
Elphberg of them all". Backed by the studio orchestra,
Cheap sentiments hold their potency across the years.

The best exits....... Not for you the pension and the garden,
Long years' confusion in the geriatric ward,
The grey-faced quietus in the hospice bed.
Rather the sudden shock of hero's rapier thrust,
The rapturous kiss behind THE END, the burst of laughter
At the joker's final prank, the impudent salute -
"Au revoir, play-actor!" - and the slow-motion dive
Into the castle moat. Goodbye, goodbye.

You're better out of it, I feel. What have you to do
With ambiguous anti-heroes, ruthless Bonds,
Obsessed fanatics and dysfunctional cops?
How can boots and rapier avail against the suicide bomb,
The serial killer, shock and awe?

Buckle your swashes tight and still remain
In Ruritania, Sherwood and the Spanish Main.
Perhaps in better days your time will come again.

Hello My Lovely

I got back to the office late.
She was already sitting there;
my old armchair glowed as if
it couldn't believe its luck.
The way she'd crossed her legs
reminded the lazy frog in my throat
of its licence to jump.
Her eyes were blue-chip pools of ice-water
that mirrored dancing fires of lust.
"Marlowe," she purred. Her voice cut through me
like a chocolate-malted laser beam.
"How can I persuade you to take this job?".............

I went out on the sidewalk,
my knees doing a jazz number on bass
and drums, and called a cab.
"WalMart on Second," I told the hackie.
Her eyes were dark pools of Bovril
on a marble worktop.
"Marlowe," she husked. Her words licked into my ears
like yoghurt on jello.
"Shall I pull over?"..........

I entered the store, my head blowing
trumpet riffs in a smoky cellar.
"Show me your pastrami," I said
to the dame on shelf-packing.
Her eyes were twin pools of green light
signalling Proceed Without Caution.
"Marlowe," she throated. Her tones reminded me
of honey and ice-cream in a silver scoop.
"I can show you the whole deli.".........

I got back to the apartment late,
my stomach jumping to a jive sextet;
I felt like I was covered in dairy products.
I headed for the shower.
Too late.
Her eyes were deep pools of espresso
in an all-night Starbucks.
"Marlowe," she whispered.........

Croque Monsieur

This song is sung by the writer, Greg Buchanan, in the middle of the first act of the musical, Byres Road Nights, outside the Positano Pizzeria.

Intro. *It's getting to be that season*
   In the early spring of the year;
   The rose is the symbol, the heart is the reason,
   Love must be nimble and wary of treason,
   And speak out loud and clear.

I looked in the morning paper
When I got out of bed,
And there were the Valentine messages
Across the double spread.
The usual protestations
Of sighing, undying passion,
Anonymous declarations
In a sentimental fashion.

  For Pookums still loves his Cuddles
  And Snookums is mad about Podge,
  While Milkmaid gets into muddles
  Without her Farmer Hodge.
  Frodo is yearning for Sam,
  And Gandalf blows kisses to Prue,
  Miss Bennett has hots for Darcy
  And Bigbum will always be true.

But there were two names that were missing,
Names that I looked for in vain.......
 Names that re-echo with bliss in
 My longing hopeful ears,
 Holding the mem'ry of many a kiss in
 The distance of the years......
Names for the parted lovers
Who may never meet again.

Where are you, my Croque Monsieur?
Do you think about Sunny Side Up,
And the days together, alas too few,
When our love was a brimming cup?

We met in a breakfast bistro
On the Boulevard Saint-Michel.
Your croque-monsieur was overdone
And my eggs were frazzled to hell.
You said, We'll always have Paris,
Striking a movie pose,
But little we thought that our film would end,
Each of us losing a beautiful friend
In a *Casablanca* close.

    Bunny is mindful of Froggie,
    Miss Whiplash is oiling her thong,
    Mister Spock is rocking for Jock
    And ironing his sarong.
    Abelard from East Kilbride
    Still sighs for Heloise,
    And what Paolo suggests to Francesca
    Would make her go weak at the knees.

I scanned the *Herald* pages
With something akin to despair,
Until at the bottom I suddenly saw it
And could hardly believe it was there.

"A loving thought to Sunny Side Up
From a constant Croque Monsieur -
Can we meet some day
In the old café
And study the lunch menu?"

    Hamish is faithful to Plummy,
    And Mogs loves Bangers and Stu,
    While Sunny Side Up feels warm in his tummy
    Just thinking of Croque Monsieur.

"Dear Croque Monsieur,
Your Sunny Side Up
Will always be steadfast, always be true.
The Valentine message is always new,
I.....love......you."

Croque-monsieur is a toasted sandwich of ham and cheese.

Beltane

An ancient Celtic festival

How did the horned god announce his arrival?
Clannad's breathy notes
served for the hooded man.
Where did the Druid stub his mistletoe?
The standing stones have much
to answer for.
On the night of fire and lust
the ash tree is burnt out.

celebrated at the beginning of May

May Day, May Day.
The people's flag is deepest red.
M'aidez, m'aidez.
The workers' cause is done and dead
upon New Labour's barricades.
Un pueblo unido
No será jamás vencido.

Wash my face with dew, my dear,
for I'm to be queen for a day,
and wake me early, sister fear,
for the wolf is on his way.

usually on the first day of the month (Old Style)

I love "old style",
Palladian rather than Gothic,
'Greek' Thomson, not CRM,
frock coats and Empire décolleté,
riding boots, floppy hats,
bows and cravats.
Give us back our eleven days.
April has ten more days to run
before Beltane lights up our dusk.

a Scottish quarter day, along with Lammas, Hallowmas and Candlemas

A mingy lot, the Scotch,
measuring out their days in quarters.
Give us whole days
in the good old fashion,
twenty-four hours for all
that needs to be done,
drinking and singing,
feasting and houghmagandie,
and a good fire besides.

Bonfires are often lit on the hillsides.

Tonight, all are welcome.
This Beltane,
Lord Pitmirkie will lavishly entertain.
A stirk will be roasted
in the flames
for all to partake.
There will be dancing and the usual
ceremonies.
Through the wicker frame
of his place of surveillance,
Strathclyde's finest
will take note of serious offences,
including
the abuse of regulated substances,
with associated dealing,
public drunkenness,
the unauthorised exchange of fluids,
illegal busking,
the making of excessive noise
after the hour of eleven pm,
and arson
of an aggravated kind.

Once Upon a Time in Orcadia

Of course that was only a beginning,
A new Age of Middle-Earth. After the reign of Sauron
Was ended, and Aragorn the Simpleminded ruled
In Gondor with his feudal nonsense;
After the smug High Kindred took their ships
West over sea, while the hobbits in their Shire
Were steeping their hairy feet in ale and baccy,
There were indeed dark times in Mordor.

The mines were shut, the troops dismissed,
Fresh meat a memory, all light and power cut off,
The arrogant occupying victors hunting down
The Dark Power's agents in their deepest caves.
No orc was safe from insult, violence and death,
Our language mocked, our culture crushed,
Our pride in being Orkish turned to dust
Under an alien Coalition's weight.

Just when it seemed that all was lost,
And orcs must face eternal dark-skinned slavery,
Salvation came in words of fire
Out of the Crack of Doom into the ears
Of Shagrat, chosen vessel of the Lord,
Who wrote the Precious Book of Gollum
The Martyr, final Bearer of the Ring
That in the Darkness binds us.

So in these words we triumph,
Sweeping the Rider from his silvered saddle,
Sealing the Dwarf within his jewelled cavern,
Stifling the Hobbit in his hillside burrow,
Reducing pale Gondor's towers to bloody rubble -
"There is no Lord but Gollum
And Shagrat is His Prophet.
Now is the Holy War of Orcs."

And with the new-found oil of Mordor
What cannot we achieve?

The Communication

I have read your letter,
    overlooking the unconventional
        (not to say startling)
            manner of its delivery,

Slitting open the curiously
    decorated envelope
        and withdrawing the single sheet
            of minutely executed text,

Deciphering the exotic handwriting
    in that distinctly Celtic script,
        despite the aesthetically repellent
            viridian-tinted ink,

Pocketing with an abstracted air
    both that faded photograph
        and the high-denomination banknote
            that are so thoughtfully enclosed,

Absorbing the ambiguously-phrased
    grammatically complex
        structures of its contents, and that
            subtlest whiff of menace,

Pausing to re-read and meditate
    upon the amazing revelation held
        implicitly within the brief yet
            elegant final paragraph,

Followed by the bold and flowing,
    almost indecipherable,
        swirls and curlicues
            of your familiar signature.

Such letters are not answered hastily,
    and so forgive what might appear
        to be an inconsiderate delay
            in my eventual reply,

Yet rest assured that even if these present
      non-committal utterances,
            for all their well-intentioned blandness,
              are not what you desire,

Your real concerns will soon and aptly be resolved,
      though at a time and place
           and in a manner you may find
              most disconcerting.

For now, sincerest salutations and farewell.
      In contacting me in this traditional manner
           you have done the right thing. After all,
              what are friends for?

Losing Face

His friends and family were quite adamant,
His face was sacrosanct, no images
On canvas, print or screen could show him
To the wider world. Only his words,
His deeds, his real significance
Should stand for him in history's
Long judgmental record.

Of course, some damage had been
Already done. The snaps of boyhood,
Graduation photos, wedding album,
Newspaper files on an up-and coming
Businessman, soldier, politician, author –
All had to be culled, suppressed, destroyed.
The daubs and sketches of artistic
Friends, cartoonists' squibs,
TV interviews, election posters,
They too were sent into the flames
Kindled by a zealous following.

At last, however, it was finished.
No record anywhere. None could
Point to this or that to refresh a fading
Memory. And in time the personal
Recollections also went into the fires.

No one now to say, *Yes, he could smile,*
Or, *Women found him attractive,*
Or even, *Under that beard*
His chin was slightly weak.

The myths took over.
Who dare challenge these,
The hagiography, the miracles,
The prophecies,
The lies?

American Cross Code

All across the USA
From Manhattan Island to Frisco Bay,
You'll find two friends on each city corner,
One an encourager, the other a warner,
Helping you cross the busy street,
Keeping control of your itchy feet.

Running White Man tells you to go,
Halting the traffic's urgent flow;
Cab and limo and mean machine
Slide to a halt when his shape is seen.
But watch for the drivers doing a right
In a sneaky move against the light.

Then Red Big Hand steps in to be reckoned
Counting you down with each flashing second;
Even before you're fully across,
He's telling you he's now the boss,
And holds you up with his crimson palm
As if to say, Keep still, stay calm.

New York swings from Side to Side,
Chicago has streets about half a mile wide,
Washington cars are official and proud,
LA and Frisco are way out and loud;
But heed your friends all over the land,
Running White Man and Red Big Hand,
And safely walk through the USA,
Surviving to walk another day.

Class Outline

In the old days
you knew where you were with people.
There were the ones who lived
in the posh streets,
villas and semi-detacheds,
bungalows and town houses,
your sort.
There were those who lived less outwardly,
terraces and tenement flats,
courts and cottages,
respectable to the core,
I suppose.
And then there were the less fortunate,
council estates, caravans,
prefabs, that type of thing.
The addresses gave the game away
most of the time,
the streets, the postal codes,
the house names and numbers.
It was pretty clear
if you had the eyes to see.

But now, good heavens,
who are these e-mail people?
Where do they come from,
how do we know if they're the right sort?
Their addresses merely confuse.
What is a .com person?
Sounds rather lowly station, even humble,
tradesman's entrance and all that.
And .co.uk, what's that all about?
Somebody in trade, rather unseemly
to be waving the patriotic banner.
Then there's .ac.uk, they tell me
it stands for 'academic',
terribly worthy, I've no doubt,
but what a bore.
And as for .net, I give up,
I think they let anyone in,
the odds and sods,
a multitude of plebs.
It's not my kind of world any more.
It's just not my world any more.

On the Wireless

Listen,
you back there,
sitting in your car,
doing the hoovering,
reading the morning paper,
can you hear us,
just below the rock rhythms,
off to the edge of Radio Gaga,
Hardsell Channel, Station Dumbo,
that small voice - simply talking.
No, this is not an interview,
not ads, not the three-minute news,
not a bag of soundbites,
not an ego monologue
or a dialogue of the deaf;
this is your actual rational discourse.
Been a long time, eh?
Real sentences, the full works,
relative pronouns, dependent clauses,
even the odd subjunctive.
That's rhetoric, man, the voice of reason.
Subjects?
Whatever the world
may hold of interest
to the enquiring mind
we can provide.
But, careful, there are those,
we shall not name them,
yet you know who,
are out to get us,
so do not be surprised
if the sound should fade,
the white noise swell to a peak,
the neighbouring channels
encroach and overwhelm
our modest undemanding tones.
You will not find us easily again.
Only by random twiddling,
unguided edging slowly
through the bands intently
probing for that utterly

unique phenomenon, a normal
speaking voice, will we once more
make that longed-for contact
that signifies the truly human
civilised achievement
of one mind meeting many others.

POTUS Moment

That is the pose to fix the icon,
arms out from the sides, supporting weight,
clenched fists on the desktop,
head down, viewed from the rear,
silhouette against the Oval Office window.

Familiar in Life-Magazine black and white,
the burdened democrat (actually an attempt
to relieve back pain).
Again in mono, behind the opening credits,
the anguished liberal (really an ageing actor
earning his bread).

Make it your pose too, just as false.
Super-delusions - free world leader,
winning the war on terror, business Big Brother,
doing God's work. Head of troubled Jove,
Atlantean shoulders, fists of Rocky.
Yet can you sense the pain, pretence
and dumb bewilderment -
How did it come to this?

The Irruption of Topsy

Five Siamese cats, all black, white and grey,
Once lived in a mansion in Grantown-on-Spey;
There was Kirsty and Squeegee and Goober and Mouse,
And Chula, the eldest, was head of the house.
They existed together in absolute bliss,
There was never a spit, there was never a hiss;
They placidly slept, ate and washed side by side,
You never saw any cats more dignified.
But all this exploded in mighty furore
When Topsy the Spider Cat came to the door.
She was small, she was striped, she was utterly twee,
She hadn't a trace of high-class pedigree.
She wormed her way in without shred of excuse
And subjected the inmates to vulgar abuse.
She ate from their dishes and slept on their chairs,
She pee'ed in their boxes and chased them upstairs.
It wasn't too long before each Siamese
Was bewailing the loss of their comfort and ease
They debated on ways to escape the intruder
And Chula proclaimed he would imitate Buddha.
He studied his navel in true Eastern manner
And finally entered the feline Nirvana.
Kirsty went walkabout in a great hurry
And contracted liaisons throughout Nairn and Moray.
The whole sordid business so affected poor Goober
That he hijacked a Boeing and flew it to Cuba.
While the last that was heard of our dear friend, young Squeegee,
He was catching the rats on a slow boat to Fiji.
And Mouse took a fit of acute perturbation,
Which led to his going into deep hibernation.
But the cause, little Topsy, has taken her leave
And the five Siamese cats no longer need grieve.
In fact, as I hear, in a very short while,
They can enter retreat on a croft on Black Isle.

(Written for Jean and Catriona in 1976)

What the Ancients Did for Us - The Picts

My goodness, where can one begin? All the wonderful ideas and inventions that this talented people developed and passed down to us. We owe so much to them. In their little corner of the northern world, the Picts were a crucible of creativity. We might go as far as to say that civilisation would look very different without their massive contribution. They were truly among the inventors of the modern world.

Paint, for instance......
The Painted Men, as Tacitus, was it, termed them - those bright-hued warriors across the dripping moor, shaking their iron axes, terrifying to enemies in polychromatic nakedness, tattoos and swirly lines, piercings and danglies. Their artistry astounds. And do we not see them still - the faces all flags and funny cats and dogs, the warpaint makeup; mermaids and daggers on biceps and butterflies on bums; boxers and mudwrestlers, streakers and naturists. Thank you, Picts.

And architecture too.....
What a breakthrough that was! Enough of turf and heather, let's use stone for building. After all, we're loaded with the stuff. And so the first small step for men from brochs on the headlands to castles and cathedrals and erotic gherkins, from inscribed and symbol-dripping standing stones to a billion gravestones and war-memorials and birdcrapped statues. *Calgacus, nos morituri te salutamus!*

The matriarchal society......
What's to say? Mother-in-law jokes, *Hail Mary full of grace*, the other Madonna, Spice Girls, and, of course, our own dear Queen.

A strong navy......
Not a lot of people know that. Rule of the seas from Pentland Firth to Pittenweem, from Orkney to Oronsay (at least until the Norskis happened along). From small acorns do mighty hearts of oak arise - Nelson breaking the French line at Trafalgar, *"There's something the matter with our bloody ships today"*, the Falklands Task Force and the U.S. Sixth Fleet. Pity about the peat-burning submarine, though.

But not your language.........
Enigmatic words and names on mossy stones. P-Celt or Q-Celt, or even proto-Celt? Who knows, who will ever know? This is what you never really did for us - give us your histories at first hand, your songs and laws

and novels and users' handbooks for Dark Age microwaves and plasma-screen tellies. Your philosophies and How To Get Rich self-help books. Without a language, a people dies from the earth. We should know.

And the best thing you did for us was not give us your religion.......
More than enough of them from other arrogant and credulous sources. Thank you, thank you, thank you.

The Seer of Achnashellach Contemplates Religion
From The Sayings of Seumas, Chapter II, verses 1 - 10.

1. A great day shall come; and it shall be a day of warm sun with occasional cloud and a few scattered showers from the west that will refresh every croft and garden;

2. And on that day the holy books shall be returned overdue to the library, and everybody's ticket shall be lost.

3. The voices of Allah and Jehovah and God the Father, Son and Holy Ghost shall echo in ever-diminishing cadence down to an ultimate burp;

4. The knives of mutilation shall be transformed into potato-peelers; the thunderbolt of Jehovah and the sword of the Prophet and the Tridents of Christ's Church Militant shall be reduced to Action Man toys; various clerics and purveyors of pious, ponderous, violent or pawky nothings will form an orderly queue at the local Job Centre;

5. The hejab and the chador and the burqa shall blow away in the wind to amaze and perturb the passing seabirds; the hair of the freed women shall stream through every square and the glow of their faces shall radiate in every street.

6. Every church and cathedral and mosque and synagogue shall become a lodging for the homeless, a cafe for the hungry, a pub for the thirsty, a school for the ignorant, or a care-home for abandoned pets.

7. All beards shall be shaved, all locks shall be given fashionable haircuts, all ritual accessories shall be exchanged for Marks and Spencer vouchers.

8. And all people shall come together and join in the harmonious consumption of bacon rolls, accompanied by a glass or two of a good New World Chardonnay;

9. There shall be selected readings from William Blake, and some rousing choruses of "A man's a man for a' that";

10. And much nonsense shall finally perish from the earth.

Creationists Ahoy!

Here they come again like bugs,
out from under their stones,
just when we thought they'd gone to ground
with the manure and the mouldy bones,

ousted by reason, baffled by science
and incontrovertible fact,
dispatched with their cruel delusions,
dismissed, exploded and sacked.

Yet up they rise from the know-nothing bogs
raising their banners on high,
proclaiming the old-time religion
with the same old pig-headed cry:

"Down with Darwin, down with Science,
this Evolution's absurd!
What ain't in the Bible's a God-damned libel
on Heaven's infallible word.

"Down with Enlightenment, down with Reason,
pack them all off to Hell!
We've got the President, got the Congress,
and we're going to get you as well."

So set up the nonsense academies,
endow a claptrap college,
deprive the kids of their right to the truth,
selling Faith instead of Knowledge.

Pretend you can cancel out the years,
turning the clock right back,
binding women and children in servitude
to the vain old men in black.

We can tell you now it'll never wash,
however you splutter and blether.
Facts are chiels that winna ding
and you can't hold up the weather.

You can fool some people some of the time
and yourselves your whole life through,
but the Universe sings to a different air
and its song has no part for you.

From the Pictish Phrase-book

Beware, your mother-in-law is observing us from the gazebo.

Excuse my importunity but is there a seller of sponges in this village?

Can you direct me to a non-circular hotel?

I appear to have trodden in some ferret-manure.

Thank you, I have enough porridge for the moment.

This is not the same cutlery that I used at breakfast.

Ladies, you are mistaken, this is not your bedchamber.

I think you will find that all the wheels should be of equal size.

Is that your father-in-law at the window of the gun-room?

Excuse me, I have an urgent appointment with the village tattoo-remover.

I should of course love to join in the dance, but my sword is rather blunt.

More from the Pictish Phrase-book

Sir, I feel your wolfhound is becoming overly affectionate.

This is truly a fine necklace, madam. Your husbands clearly took great care of their teeth.

So what is the purpose of these deep holes in the floor?

Did your daughter really mean to eat the Harry Potter book I gave her?

Surely these are not bones down there at the bottom?

Pray tell me why no buses run in alternate months.

Yes, I shall descend this ladder if you insist.

I should prefer my ice-cream without mustard if you don't mind.

Do you really need this ladder elsewhere? I may need it to re-ascend.

Please tell room service I do not require the sheep's liver to be actually removed and cooked in my presence.

I am sorry you feel you must go.

It is, I fear, getting rather dark down here.

Grail Quest

Let's see if I've got this quite right.
You're looking for a drinking cup,
Not just any old cup that might
Be used on days the lads are up

In town for races and some fun,
But one particular which sat
On table for the Galilean
Party that reserved a room at

Passover weeks ago, I can't
Remember clearly why or when,
A bunch of scruff, the type who'll rant
Along the streets, some fishermen,

A shepherd maybe, real rough trade,
Come to the city to make trouble,
Believe me, not at all afraid
Of Roman lawcourts, just a rabble.

That crazy preacher was among
Them, whom the Romans nailed to cross,
Judas, the guy that ended hung,
And Simon, who's become their boss.

Anyway, this cup, you want the one
The preacher used to give the toast,
Whatever, who knows what the man
Was doing? There must be a host

Of differing views, considering who
Were present. I could fetch a cup
And say "This is the one for you",
But I'd be making something up.

The fact is, what with dopey Jonah
Doing the washing-up, last week's
Big wedding - look, I'm not a moaner,
But what do you expect from Greeks? -

The turnover in cups and bowls
Has been horrendous just of late.
My potter's bill alone makes holes
In my accounts, I tell you straight.

My best advice to you comes free.
Pop down the road to Simeon's shop
And order his big specialty,
A *Goblet de Luxe*, with every stop

Pulled out to give it eye-appeal,
Bright paint, big handles, knobbly bits,
The tourists think they've got a deal,
It really dazzles when it sits

In state upon a Roman table.
Even better, if you've what's required,
I know a man supremely able,
Not cheap but everywhere admired,

Whose work in silver's really swish.
He'll do a chalice, fine engraved
With all the symbols that you wish,
Any image that is craved.

And if you like, I'd write a line
'Confirming' it's the kosher item.
I'd add some blurb about the wine,
Our own house red, and not to spite 'em,

I'd fatten out the provenance,
Eye-witness statements, sworn and sealed,
Some affidavits, covenants,
All heavy-duty stuff to wield

In any courtroom. You can make
Some fools believe in anything -
A cup, some bits of cloth, a fake
Effect with lights, a choir to sing

Pretentious words, in Greek maybe,
And bingo! you're away in style,
A myth to gull eternity,
To puzzle scholars and beguile

The superstitious ages still
Unborn. And we shall both come in
To big-time bucks. Trust me it will
Be so, for I am Doctor Spin.

Sorry, Chaps

(A spokesman for the Scottish Landowners has suggested that they might consider apologising to the Scottish people for the Highland Clearances.)

"Being a laird means never knowing how to say sorry."

We're sorry the Clearances happened,
We regret that they ever occurred.
Driving you off to the ends of the earth
Was a faux pas just too, too absurd.

We're sorry the Clearances happened,
It was really just meant as a joke.
One moment your clachans were standing,
The next, they were going up in smoke.

We're sorry the Clearances happened,
We hope you can now understand.
We wanted some wool for a sweater
And it all got a bit out of hand.

We're sorry the Clearances happened,
It's just that we hadn't a sou,
Till the accountants came up with a smashing wheeze
For making things tickety-boo.

We're sorry the Clearances happened,
It's a pity you didn't object.
But you all spoke that weird Teuchter lingo
So your feelings were hard to detect.

We're sorry the Clearances happened
And you had to live down by the sea.
But we're sure you can look on the bright side
And do a good cheap B and B.

We're sorry the Clearances happened
And the emigrant ships sailed away.
But we think it turned out for the best
Seeing the rugger your grandkids can play.

We're sorry the Clearances happened,
But it's all part of Nature's great scheme.
We now to the hills can lift our eyes
Where our deer and our grouse roam supreme.

We're sorry the Clearances happened,
But we don't intend being dispossessed,
Since we after all are conserving the land
And jolly well know what is best.

We're sorry the Clearances happened,
But, like you, we're all patriots stout,
And we'll stand firm upon our green wellies,
Till we sell to some Arab or Kraut.

Monarchs of the Glen

The people of the Highlands, it pains me to say it, do not possess their own land.
It may have been Finlay who left the Beefeater gin bottle in the ha-ha.
Torquil, they tell me, writes occasional letters to the *Daily Telegraph*.
Strictly speaking, there are no lairds in the Highlands.
Kirsty, you might say, drives her Range Rover like a bat out of hell.
Morag, paradoxically, holds holistic healing sessions in the Lodge Cottage.
Every estate has a proprietor (human or corporate).
Shona, I have heard, was Head Girl at Cheltenham Ladies College.
It was probably Fergus who cleaned his Purdeys on the kitchen table.
Caledonia, stern and wild, fit nurse for Melancholy's child.
Fiona, strange to say, has opened a craft boutique beside the Estate Office.
Catriona, we believe, has had a thing with a Cambridge Rugger Blue.
Things are, however, beginning slowly to change.
It was certainly Farquhar who drove home sozzled from the Village Games.
Rory has sometimes toyed with the notion of learning Gaelic.
From scenes like these Auld Scotia's grandeur springs.

Welcome

Welcome to this land.
  Welcome to you all -
you plumbers and cleaners,
  doctors and nurses,
    busdrivers and shopkeepers,
      students and language-learners,
chefs and restaurateurs,
  checkout ladies, shelfstackers,
    assemblers and mechanics,
      diggers, shovellers, fruitpickers,
mothers with baby buggies,
  housewives with polybags,
    fathers with mobiles,
      children with wide eyes -
welcome to you whatever your land.

And thank you for coming,
  for your skills and your ideals,
  for your smiles and your optimism,
    for putting up with our insults and assaults,
      for doing the jobs we don't want,
for making our streets more colourful,
  our buses more polyglot,
    our cuisine more interesting,
      our minds more open.

We need you, oh how we need you.
  Keep on coming.

Symposium in the Park with George
(George Elder Davie, died 20/03/07)

Philosophy? - you mean, for everyone?
But we disposed of that years ago in favour of sociology.

Democracy? - yes, we already give all pupils the same curriculum,
though there will always be necessary hierarchies.

Intellect? - we prefer to ensure that all teachers are trained
in the best techniques, so how much they actually know is irrelevant.

A Scottish education? - Ah, there our students are well prepared
for the culture of Scotland – MacJobs and debt management.

The Democratic Intellect? Still seems like a good idea to me.
Worth trying some day.

Social Education Period

How do you make a Republican?
Here is how one was formed.

It was to be a great National day
that Coronation June, the Service
in Saint Giles', giving the Scots
a little sense of sharing London's
glitter. Thus the Honours
brought from the Castle Tower,
the peerage and the provosts,
professors and the like, douce
bourgeois Scotland's representatives,
with, tucked in neatly, Scotland's Future,
Head Boys and Girls from the Academies.
"Truly an honour to the school," said
Rector Lodge to me and Moira
in his panelled office with the crests.

There was a slight problem getting in,
persuading a Highland polis
to admit me under the rope,
flashing my gold-edged invite,
the main entrance seemingly reserved
for dignitaries in taxis or in limos,
not for sweating teenager in a
tweedy Burton suit.

But, once inside, surely it was
all worthwhile. Stained glass
and organ voluntaries, the morning suits
and special frocks, the Royal Company
of Archers, Knights of the Thistle,
in swish robes and velvet hats.
The Sword of State borne by a skeletal peer,
the Crown on cushion carried
by a sober-for-that-morning duke,
and other bits and pieces
of some ritual significance.
And then, the Queen
herself, young and newly-crowned,
honouring her faithful Scottish subjects
with her Gracious Presence.

And, yes, it was a nice hat. Every
woman said so. The dress cut
with such taste in the slightly passé
New Look style. And, oh, the handbag,
must have cost a bomb in Bond Street.
Her Majesty was well turned out,
a lovely photo for the Tatler.
Just the right note to strike,
enough to comment on, but not
to let those Scots believe they were
being taken seriously as a nation.

Did I feel a let-down then?
Probably, but memory dwines down
towards self-justifying myth.
Yet I am certain that June day
formed, not just in me, the cast of mind
that, ever since, has had no time
for yonder trite and trivial woman
and her unmeriting ridiculous family.

Republic! Bring it on, say I.
Or else take every Derby winner
with his fine rosette
and well-bred snuffle;
crown him King for the year,
a fitting monarch for the fond
and fawning, Royalty-adoring,
top-hat-doffing,
pearls and twin-set coterie.

Royal Wedding

So here we go again, the Abbey or
Saint Pauls, demure princesses under veils,
those yah-yah princelings togged as if for war,
pretending Scottish roots, a love of Wales.

New tawdry fictions hyped by media guile
to cloak them in a spurious relevance
and push their creaking coach another mile
through history's ironic resonance.

Drag out the awful uncles, horsey aunt,
the leathery step-mum and a weirdo dad,
a dimbo brother, Granny Grim and gaunt
old Grandpa – for a day, forget that sad

elusive, unattainable it seems,
enlightened fair republic of our dreams.

BBC Weather Map

And now the weather.

Here is your weather from the BBC
where you are up top..
Just to be clear, folks,
look at the map, this is your country.
See, we have conveniently shrunk it
to put you in your place,
a little bigger than Wales or that Northern Ireland
(They are really below the level of significance),
but you need a special treatment.

Here is England as we know it,
rather different from the impression
given by STV or the major world atlases.
The South-West and the Home Counties claim
their true important place
in Britain's political reality.

There you are, chaps,
snow in the glens, rain in the Central Belt,
high winds in the east.
Get used to it.
Serves you right.
Enjoy the rest of your evening.

Watershed

Would you recognise the moment
when it comes, all at once, perhaps
as you are sitting at table, talking
of trivial matters, smiling,
sipping coffee or just quietly
looking at each other's faces?

I do not mean "the moment of truth",
nor yet "the breaking point", far less
"decision time" or "the point of no return".

It is that second when a shift in tone,
a sudden sideways glance, withdrawal
of a hand, a smile when no smile should be,
in a second fractionally longer than a second,

tells you that what you had securely
thought was safe, established, part of your life
that you could count upon, has begun to slip,
may be for a time stilled with conscious effort,
anchored with failing hooks and grapnels,
saved and saved again with desperate hope,
increasing rancour, but, being honest,
is now, this very moment, upon the skids,
headed for the tubes,
effectively over.

Perfect Image

Strolling this summer evening in the city,
I count my blessings as a man of worth.
My business flourishes, my health is pretty
Good for someone of my age and girth.

My modest wife discreetly walks behind,
In sober blacks, appropriately veiled;
My two sons do what young men are inclined
To do these days; my daughters are curtailed

By dutiful obedience to me
And keep within the home, when not at school.
The doors are locked, and I possess the key.
They know it's for their good that I should rule.

This is a sick society in which
We have to live, and thus we keep apart,
Holding our values. So I may grow rich
And yet maintain my purity of heart.

I have my doubts about what schools here peddle,
Encouraging the young to disbelieve
The truths we stand by. Girls should never meddle
Beyond the basics. That would be to weave

A prickly dress of thorns for all. If taught,
They'd want to choose their lives, come from their shell,
Unlike my wife, who knows her place. She's got
The message, veils conceal her bruises well.

My daughters now are of an age to marry,
And properly prepared by skilful knives.
This summer, single flights back home will carry
Both as cousins' designated wives.

I doubt if they'll complain. Last month I took
The family to see a poor blind aunt
Who lives alone, since long ago she took
The wrong path. Sad to see how acid can't

Be gentle as an instrument of honour.
My faithless sister had a fairer face;
She brought her own doom down upon her.
My brother-in-law may know her resting-place.

All such stern forms of justice I uphold.
Discovering my mother's brief affair,
I told on her before her sin was cold,
And watched her stoning in the public square.

Strolling this summer evening in the sun,
I pride myself on my integrity;
Father, husband, giving place to none,

Perfect
      Image of
            Good -
                  P.I.G.

Muckin Oot the Auld Hame.

Faith, sic a boorach yir in the noo, aa this stuff in yir hoose,
Theres a wheen uv brucks beneath yir feet ah kin see ur uv nae mair use.
Leave it tae wis, the specialists, the boys ae the scaffie squad,
It ull aa gang on the dust-cairt when yis gie the approvin nod.

Whit aboot this fitba junk, yer fur dumpin the lot, ah hope,
Its stunted yir minds fur a hunner year, as bad as smokin dope,
The auld firm programmes, the telly chat, the drivellin sports page pap,
The strips an trophies, the scarves an tee-shirts, the chants an souvenir crap?

Awa wi it, fine, an ah tell yis tae, while oor on the declutterin job,
Oo kin stick this pape and proddy cant deep in the lorrys gob.
The flags ae the ludge, the bowler hats, the flute an fenian bands,
The separate schules, the halie blethers, ahl tak them aa aff yir hands.

Ma goad, heres an unco sicht, whit a load ae trash in yir cellar,
Wee Scottie dugs an tartan doilies an records ae Kenneth McKellar,
 Div yis hae nae taste, ah ask yis, sprigs ae white heather indeed,
Auld Sunday Posts an the Daily Record, is this aa yis kin read?

An look, fur peety sake, at yon pile ae bottles an cans.
Ahd say yiv a heap ae problems there, an no jist recyclin wans.
Get rid ae the drams, the pint-an-a-nips, the skoals an the slainte mhaths,
The staggers, the punch-ups, the boakt-up pizzas, the stinkin pee on the
waas.

Up in the attic here ah see piled mony a lang-deid notion,
Whirlies ae dust obscurin the licht, perpetual clichés in motion,
*Here's tae us wha's like us, oh flower of scotland, we're a' jock tamson's
bairns,*
Clyde-built, coothie, fur auld lang syne - stanes on crumblin cairns.

Yir a collector ae history buiks, ah note, heres mony a foosty tome,
Union betrayal, Bonnie Prince Chairlie, Geneva's tussle wi Rome.
Puir auld Scotland gubbed again, aw! the romantic blether,
Its anither clearance yir needin noo, alang wi the bracken an heather.

* * * * * *

There yis ur, its a great wee hoose noo that aa the rubbish has went.
Yiv got space fur improvin and DIY, plus room fur enlightenment.

Cycle Puncture

.... The spring, the summer,
The childing autumn, angry winter, change
Their wonted liveries, and the mazed world,
By that increase, now knows not which is which.
And this same progeny of evil comes
From our debate, from our dissension.
(A MIDSUMMER NIGHT'S DREAM, ACT 2, SC.1, LINES 111-116)

So it's come round to spring again.
I marvel it dares show its face
After last year's fiasco, when
The shrunken reservoirs froze over
And April's showers dropped hillsides
On a dozen roads. The flooded city
And the shattered coasts lie far beyond
Our local ken but scar our hearts.

It must have been the summer
That began to set the pattern.
All those forest blazes, not in distant Oz
But down our Highland bens,
Along our Border trails; the too
Unseasonable gales that swept
Whole families away
On Hebridean isles.

And autumn, season of mists,
Transformed to over-brilliant Indian
Summer, did we think it normal
That the colours of the fall
Should be accompanied by gorgeous
Flush of blooms, the scent of lilac,
Mowing of lawns on Halloween?
Fireworks in the perfumed evening air.

Last winter, I remember, Christmas
Was no dream in white, New Year
Smiled in mild benevolence,
And startled roses pushed
Their shoots into the February sun.
March heard a fleeting wintry moan,
A blip of blizzard, sudden melt,
And sunny days returned.

And now, it's spring, the sweet spring.
Where are the snowdrops of yesteryear?
The fluttering, dancing daffs delayed,
No pretty maids all in a ring.
The voice of the turtle ne'er heard in the land,
And young man's fancy nightly spurns
The hots of love.
Cuckoo, jug jug, pu-we, tuwittawoo.

The Sea, The Sea

How can I have failed to see this all these years?
The coming tide by Murdo's burn,
Swirling seaweed at Stromeferry pier,
The St Clair's hissing wake up Bressay Sound,
Baltic bright behind the cruise ship sun-deck,
Slick wet sea-lions on their Frisco Bay pontoons,
The beach at Luskentyre, nothing until America,
Those bright perspectives west across
Atlantic or Pacific blank immensity.

Has it taken seventy years and more
To realise that this is all one,
The same expanse, the same enormous glassful,
Drawn from the tap in Glasgow,
Swigged from the plastic bottle,
Drunk from the hand in hillside springs,
Raised from the ocean's breast,
Swirled in clouds across fragmented lands,
Precipitated finally upon uncaring rock
To give it life, the chances to diversify and thrive,
A verdant glow concealing all the sterile underlay,
The irremediable stone?

All that we have, all that we are,
Is but the faint collateral effect
Of oceanic forces, sea's encroachment
On an alien territory by one means or another,
Currents or tides or weather patterns,
Telling us every day, should we choose to listen,
We are the children of Poseidon,
Bright spawn of Ocean, water babies,
Casual spindrift of the restless waves.

The Who

Who goes there, who goes where,
who goes down to the foot of the stair,
who goes halfers, who goes dutch,
who goes into giggles at the slightest touch,
who goes pop, who goes 'fair cop',
wha gaes aff the heid an ower the top,
who goes croak, who goes for broke,
who goes phut and up in smoke,
who's going grey, who's going astray,
who goes not home at the end of the day,
who's gone to the john, the doo-ron-ron,
away with the fairies, gone, clean gone?

Who comes here, who comes near,
who comes combing their golden hair,
who comes wi a lass, who comes to pass,
who comes up trumps at the top of the class,
who comes out in May, who comes out gay,
who comes out in spots when he kneels to pray,
who comes with a swagger, saying 'Hoots mon',
who cometh in triumph through Babylon,
who's coming to dinner, who's coming to save,
who's coming stalking back from the grave,
who came from space, the Other Place,
who came and went without a trace?

Who knows what, who knows ought,
who knows more than diddley-squat,
who knows best, who knows the rest,
who knows the answers to the final test,
who knows their place, who knows it's a race,
who knows the score and who's still in the chase,
who knows he's bidden, who knows you're kiddin,
who knows just where the bodies are hidden,
who knows a man who knows a man
who knows who to get to carry the can,
who knew all along it would end in tears,
but kept it quiet for a couple of beers?

Who comes, who goes,
we can only suppose,
but there's someone somewhere
who knows, who knows.

Catcall

I am the voice inside your head,
I am the chapter waiting to be read,
I am the secret you don't want spread,
I am the cat in the bag.

I am the rotting cheese in the fridge,
I am the troll beneath the bridge,
I am the smoke-signals high on the ridge,
I am the cat in the bag.

I am the hand that tugs your sleeve,
I am the guest who refuses to leave,
I am the bill you're going to receive,
I am the cat in the bag.

Sooner or later I'm going to appear,
Land in your lap with a snarl and a sneer,
Scratch your hand and spill your beer,
So all the neighbours will say, "Oh dear,
That's the cat out of the bag."

The Numerous Conjunction

The When of Four,
the Where of Seven,
describe the ultimate
How of Eleven.

Yet the If of Eight,
the Unless of Ten,
bring Three's Although
and Six's So
together with Nine
again and again.

Why shuts the door
on One and Five,
meeting with Two
in a low-down dive,
so that Twelve looks tense
beside Whither and Whence.

Flaubert's Crossword

Attendez, this is how it works:
the shape a skeleton
in monochrome,
its blocks and struts
defining what is needed.
I see it now before me waiting
on the clues to nudge me
to provide its flesh, the words
precise, exactly formulated
as solutions to the long parade
of puzzles, now across the line,
now down the page, filling
the template aptly,
les mots justes,
called from the mental hoard
to build the total pattern
full and eloquent -
et enfin, voilà,
Emma's latest sister,
Salammbo's newest sacrifice.

Writing

Writing is:
the sex life of stationery;
what writing does;
a strategy employed by paper to achieve world domination;
a conspiracy between the past and the present aimed at controlling the future;
the eye's secret weapon against the ear;
the cinema of the intellect;
the necessary wool for knitting a jumper of meaning;
that which "*maketh an exact man*".

there's aye Scotland
aye daonnan always
I eye mi suil I ee
future future future
ay ay ay ay ay ay
sí sí sí sí sí sí
future futur futuro
yo ojo yo ojo jo ull
always sempre siempre
hay siempre escocia

EYE TO THE FUTURE
(A Poem Sequence)

El pueblo unido no será jamás vencido.
(The people united will never be defeated)

I
Better Thegither

Aye, dearie, listen tae yir auntie,
I'm tellin ye, it's no a day fur gaein oot.
Owre mony rough weans hingin roun
Waitin tae gie ye a batterin.

Stick hame wi us, we'll tak care uv ye,
See ye hiv aw ye need, wee bit pocket-money,
Rin aboot in yir ain wee gairden,
Read Oor Wullie in the Sunday Post.

I'll mak some chips tae yir tea,
Furget thae furrin cairry-oots an cafes.
Hame's best, ye'll fin, stick tae whit ye ken.
Ye're jist no up tae the big bad warld.

Ye see, dearie, Auntie kens whit's best fur ye,
Me an Uncle Davie. Aye, we're better thegither, but.

II
Skipping Chant

Three wee doolies cam tae ma gate,
The first wis a laddie a bit ower blate,
Stanes in his pooches tae gie him some wecht
An keep him frae fleein up oot o sicht.

Three wee tumshies cam tae ma hoose,
The second wis a lassie posh-spoken an douce,
Drew a definitive line in the sand,
But the risin tide left her naewhere tae stand.

Three wee numpties cam tae ma door,
The third wis a wifie aw grumpy an soor,
Total no-no, face like fizz,
Couldnae sell scones tae yir Aunty Liz.

"Better thegither, aw safe an soun,"
Fair keen tae drive auld Scotland doun.

III
The Right Hon. PM Speaks

It's right that folk should have a major say
in how their country's run, and right indeed
that they should know their rights. All people need
a right and proper sense of worth, as may

these little nations to the right of us
(somewhere in Europe, if I'm right in thinking)
show example. Right, but still it's blinking
strange when Jocks kick up a real right fuss

about their rightful freedom, when we see
right well that they were never even slightly
wronged. At Eton I learned history rightly
in that respect. It seems quite right that we

require right-thinking Scots to all vote No.
I'm right, I know I'm right, quite right, you know.

IV
The Sleep of Reason

Another day, more threats and gibes and lies –
you'll be alone, you'll be without a friend,
you'll all be poor, unable to defend
against Fate's ills, foul weather, plagues of flies.

Another day, more gibes and lies and threats –
we'll shut your borders, stop your foreign trade,
destroy your money, see you don't get paid,
and send our heavies to collect your debts.

Another day, more lies and threats and gibes –
you're just a shower of idle drunken Jocks,
you haven't got the sense to change your socks,
you live in slums, flea-ridden clans and tribes.

Another day, a week, a month, a year –
the No-No politics of sour-mouthed fear.

V
Stop the Press

So let us praise the Scottish tabloid Press,
who fear no foe, who write the truth, who take
no bribes, who stand up free and pure, and make
the cause of Scotland theirs to fight. God bless

them aw. Weel, maybes aye, or maybes naw.
There's some wad loodly say they ate the pies,
or sellt their grannies' jerseys, tellt the lies
their London bosses wantit, did hee-haw

for Scotland, showing they'd rather dig the dirt
on Tommy, get wee Alec, write their sneers
at Holyrood, make threats and stir up fears
in blaring headlines, do their best to hurt

the present, twist the past and, worst, obstruct
the future. Time to say to them, Get knotted!

VI
The Question

Like in the poster
when the curious children cluster round,
What did you do in the War, Daddy?
and the haunted face reveals
its shame,

So in the mirror
through all those after-years
you'll catch the face that,
when they brought the Future
in a simple question,
could only answer, No.

VII
Two Views

(a)
I was brought up to be a proper Scot,
proud to be British, honouring the Queen,
stood for the Anthem, seeing no clash between
an Us and Them. I never questioned what
we learned from press and radio, never prayed
that Scotland could be better through a change.
It shocked me, seeing scoundrels rearrange
the world I knew, and in due time I made

the patriotic choice and voted No
against my country. Yet, what did it gain?
a cross on paper changed things not at all.
the land moves on, but folk I meet, although
polite, display faint flickers of disdain –
I cannot face these mirrors on my wall.

(b)
I was brought up to be a proper Scot,
proud to be British, honouring the Queen,
stood for the Anthem, seeing little clash between
an Us and Them. I only questioned what
they told us when I saw that Scotland played
always as second team. I worked for change,
and cheered to see the system rearrange
to bring a better nation. Thus I made

the only rational choice and voted Yes
for Scotland's soul. We play the cards we drew,
with deeper blue and white the saltires fly,
and unarrestably we all progress,
aware, unlike the timid, we've been true –
I can look anybody in the eye.

VIII
Primary Sources

The Inner Hebrides from north to south,
out at the map, a knuckle rap for each
one missed, Miss Wylie's sure-fire way to teach
the shapes and names of Scotland, giving mouth

to words of Gaelic, Norse and Scots, soon charged
with history by Miss MacGregor's tales,
how Bruce and Stewart win, how Wallace fails,
and ballads' mysteries, real life enlarged

to art and carried on to Scotland's songs,
Miss Turnbull leading from piano stool,
the wealth of Burns and Hogg and Nairne. That school,
these teachers – to that distant time belongs

my certainty that I can never go
out to betray their work by voting No.

IX
Interview with H.M.

Ah, Mr Cameron, please take a chair.
Can we dispense with all the usual natter?
I'm charged with telling you how much we care
About your handling of this Scottish matter.

You see, we Royals feel a special pull.
My mother read us Burns to great effect;
Charles practised Gaelic at his northern school;
For Will, the democratic intellect

Was fair the jinkies at St Andrew's Uni.
So, be assured, I wear a Scottish hat,
And though your pompous Old Etonian squads
May sneer at it as merely Brigadoon-y,
The Queen of Scots? Yes, I'd be proud as that,
As were my ancestors, against all odds.

X
Mirror Image

hiv yi bin watchin thon telly series,
oan thi noo, furget thi name,
culd be burger, means society ur sumpn,
its aw aboot this rich wee country
jist across the watter fae uz, hiz its ain
parliment n guvrment like, stauns by itsel,
theres this wumman, real smart, guid looker n aw,
shes thi prime minister, leads her party,
jiggles thi ither politicians aroon, kinna coalition,
goat this policy tae mak things better,
sort oot thi money, guid health, schules,
mak life guid fur evribody, no sae much
rich n puir, gangs aw ower thi warl tae,
europe, africa, america like, sees thi big pickcher,
global problems, ken, really coonts fur sumpn,
maks thi wee country respecktit, no a joke,
no jist a part ae a bigger place,
aw thi people there, see, believe in thirsels,
prood ae their hame, no feert ae onythin,
must be a great bit tae live, yon scotland

- culdnae happn here but, see uz danes,
cannae hack it, niver cam tae much,
pure pish, aye, pish, wir better thegither
wi big brither germany, no tae worry,
jerryll see uz richt.

XI
Ingratitude

When the good Sir James at Teba
Threw the heart of Bruce before him
Into the throng of yet-unborn Spain's enemies
And rode to death, fighting its cause,

He did not think a future Spain
Would selfishly rebuff his nation's claim,
Denying the right already won by him
And that noble heart at Bannockburn.

When a company of Scotland's common men
Joined hearts supporting Spanish freedom,
Meeting the Fascist fire on dusty hillsides,
They did not know a future Spain

Would blank their nation's entry
Into a newer International Brigade,
Making a mockery of La Pasionaria's
Outstretched arms beside the Clyde.

XII
The Human Chain – 11/09/13

It was still early when we reached the place
red-circled on our map, all seven ticked
as present – parents, grannies, kids – with strict
instructions, national headbands, sheets in case

we didn't know the words – then it was time,
hold hands, spread out across our land, a row
extending north to south, full stretch, all go
to make this Nine-Eleven one to rhyme

and sing about in coming years, the way
we outfaced post-imperial rant and whine
with airs of home and strong unbroken line
to will that Yes on referendum day.

Let this spell take, that eager people see
a time when Catalonia shall be free.

XIII
Aye, Man, Aye

Did ye think it wad aw disappear
When the votes were coontit an stacked?
Ye saved yir No-No majority
An thocht it wis settled as fact.

Wae's me ye're awa up the sheuch!
The future is no as ye thocht.
'Yes' is a word ae infinite force
An winna be hushed fur ocht.

Ye're aff oan a journey ye cannae steer,
An booked aw the wey doun the line.
The singers are up at the front ae the bus
An the driver is cheyngin the sign.

The stag has cam frae the wuid,
The eagle is circlin the rocks,
Jeannie is totally oot ae her bottle
An Jock's no gaein back in the box.

XIV
The Verdict

It's history, boys, provides the truest pleasure
to rational man. The present disappoints
with half-controlled events. Its rancorous measure,
mixing chance and bungled policies, disjoints
what future is imagined. Looking back
in calm detachment is the only way
to see how human life has found its track
through time, stumbling, blind, from day to day,
communities and nations, empires too,
that come to judgement in a patterned weave
and hang in our galactic halls for you
to learn the heights that humans may achieve.
To the defeated, History may say Alas,
but to survivors gives a Merit Pass.

Take, for example, that people who have been
my special study. Students come with me
to pace this cool side avenue and see
each portal opening up a new demesne,
a web of data-banks for each rich phase
of this land's story - First and Second King-
doms, British Interlude, that third brief fling
with monarchy before the golden days,
the settled Scots Republic that endures
into the present Northern Commonwealth.
I find its versatility and health
make it a lasting favourite and ensures
the kind continuing gaze of History
upon the threads of Scotland's tapestry.

Notes

The Broch of Glass.   Inspired by fragments of a Norse ballad, now called *The Hildina Ballad*, written down in 1774 by the Rev. George Low from the reciting of an old Foula man, William Henry. It was in the Norn tongue, the form of Norse spoken in Shetland down to the eighteenth century. The Norn original and a translation by W.G. Collingwood can be found *in A Shetland Anthology*, edited by J.J. and L.I. Graham, 1998.

In Balladia.   Scottish Ballad refs. in sequence: *Sir Patrick Spens; The Wife of Ushers Well; The Demon Lover; Tam Lin; Thomas the Rhymer (True Thomas).*

Returning to Lanark.   2011 marked the 30th anniversary of the publication of the novel, *Lanark*, by Alasdair Gray. Key motifs in the novel are: John Bunyan's *The Holy War*, the structure of the Greek Epic; and Thomas Hobbes' *Leviathan*.

Recording for Eddie.   As an 85th birthday tribute from Glasgow to the poet Edwin Morgan, the Scots Makar, 85 admirers of his work read their chosen poems of his for a presentation CD. This poem describes the experience of reading the sonnet, "A Golden Age", from Morgan's "Sonnets from Scotland". The quotation in the first line and the last two lines refer to this sonnet.

Morganstern.   The title alludes to the poet Edwin Morgan, who died in August, 2010. The poem is intended to celebrate the imaginative range and versatility of his poetic achievement.

Maighstir Norman.   2010 was the centenary of the birth of the poet, Norman MacCaig. 'Maighstir' is the Gaelic word for Master.

Day on the Hill.   The literary achievement of the Scottish writer, Neil Munro, is likened to the variety and stature of a Munro, the tallest category of Scottish mountain.

Callanish.   Callanish, with its ring of ancient stones, is on the Isle of Lewis.

Anger.   J.T. was a pupil I taught many years ago at Annan Academy. The poem deals with an experience that very many teachers will recognise.

Horatian Ode.   This poem is, like the two that follow, an elegy in memory of a dear friend and colleague. Joe O'Neill was not only a fine teacher but also a Latin and Irish Gaelic scholar. The quotation is from Horace's Odes Book I, XXII: *"The honourable man, free from vice, does not require Moorish darts or bow...."*

Remembering Jimmy.   James Inglis was a formidable scholar and teacher, deeply committed to excellence and social causes.

Lord of the Dance.   James Muir was loved by all, an enthusiast for language and books, a dedicated writer of stories and poetry. His funeral was deeply moving, made all the more so by its use of the John Barry music from the film "Dances with Wolves".

Big Guy on the Town. Ref. Frank O'Hara and his New York poems. Donald Dewar was the first First Minister of the Scottish Parliament, too soon and abruptly lost to the nation. His statue stands outside the Glasgow Royal Concert Hall.

Esperanzas. The Spanish word for 'Hopes'. The life and achievement of the Scottish traveller, writer and politician, Robert Bontine Cunninghame Graham, is at last being recognised.

King Robert IV. Although descended from the Earls of Menteith and Robert III King of Scots, Robert Cunninghame Graham was a dedicated Radical and Socialist both in and out of Parliament.

Trapalanda. In his writings, Robert Cunninghame Graham frequently mentions Trapalanda, the lost mythical city of the Indians of the pampas, a haven for horses. Graham was a personal friend of some of the artists of the Glasgow Boys school, including John Lavery and Joseph Crawhall ("Creeps"). The wild horses of the pampas ran in herds, or troops (tropillas), rounded up as needed by the Argentine Gauchos, like Exaltación Medina and Raimundo Barragán, friends of Graham in the 1870s. Gartmore was the large Cunninghame Graham estate and house in Menteith, which had to be sold in 1900 because of debts. "Chid" was Graham's nickname for his wife Gabriela, who died in 1906.

A Hero of the New World. Many Scottish people, including Highlanders, found their way to South America and a variety of new lives.

Las Cabras. The over-building and commercialisation of the south of Spain is a phenomenon of the last three decades, destroying many of the features that made it so appealing to visitors from the rest of Europe.

Boatsang. The Scots language of this translation of the first part of Pablo Neruda's *Barcarola* (*Residencia en Tierra*, 1935) is in a traditional literary mode.

Four Sonnets of Garcilaso de la Vega. Garcilaso de la Vega (c.1501-1536) was a Spanish soldier, courtier and poet, a Renaissance figure rather like Sir Philip Sidney in England, who died young fighting against the French. In his short life he wrote poetry in various forms, notably a sequence of forty sonnets in which he explored the pains and frustrations of love.

Stone Poem. This was commissioned in 2011 by Comrie Development Trust as an inscription for a standing stone to be erected at the new Cultybraggan Heritage Centre beside the village. The stone was chosen and carved by Robbie Schneider.

Sisyphus Stone. This was composed as a first draft of a possible inscription for a stone to be placed in a sculpture garden. The idea was inspired by the Greek myth of Sisyphus and is an ongoing project with Robbie Schneider.

Turn of the Season. This was commissioned by the Association for Scottish Literary Studies to accompany their annual award of Honorary Fellowships for services to Scottish Literature.

Vision. This poem was written for the Big Burns Supper Event
Competition in Dumfries, January, 2012. It was publicly displayed on a
window-pane in the Globe Inn on the High Street.

Dominus Reconstructus. How a teacher may be reincarnated to suit each
turn of educational fashion.

From the Gallery Wall. The Gainsborough portrait of the Honourable
Mrs Graham is in the National Gallery of Scotland in Edinburgh. It
was painted between 1775 and 1777 when Mary Cathcart (the second
daughter of the Earl of Cathcart) was newly married to Thomas
Graham of Balgowan. At the time of the portrait, she was in her teens.
In 1788 she met Robert Burns at the home of her brother-in-law, the
Duke of Atholle, at Blair Castle, and Burns described her in a letter
as "beautiful Mrs Graham". She contracted tuberculosis and died in
1792 aged thirty-five. Her grief-stricken husband had the portrait
put in a case and stored in a London picture-framer's back room. He
went on to have a distinguished military career, becoming one of
Wellington's generals in Spain and Portugal, and gaining the title of
Earl of Lynedoch. He lived on to the age of ninety-six, and after his
death in 1843, his heir bequeathed the portrait to the National Gallery
of Scotland on the condition that it should never leave Scotland.

Elegy on Some Gentlemen of Fortune. A memory of a lost Golden Age of
Hollywood.

Hello My Lovely. Ref. the detective novels of Raymond Chandler.

Beltane. Incidental reference is made at the end to the film, *The Wicker Man.*

Once upon a Time in Orcadia. In *The Lord of the Rings* and *The Hobbit*,
the orcs were dealt a really bad hand. With proper dental care and
dietary advice, their image could have been much more positive.

POTUS Moment. POTUS is President of the United States. The Kennedy/
West Wing pose in silhouette is now a cliché of the office.

Symposium in the Park with George. The book, *The Democratic Intellect*,
is essential reading for anyone seeking to make educational policy for
Scotland.

Social Education Period. A personal memory of June, 1953.

BBC Weather Map. A neat visual trick by our non-political BBC, reducing
Scotland by one third of its real area.

Watershed. The more I revisit this poem, the more it seems to me to be
about politics than about a failing personal relationship.

Perfect Image. A compendium of all the physical abuses visited upon
women in this male-dominated world.

Cycle Puncture. The seasonal creep associated with climate change has
produced some bizarre effects.

The Sea, The Sea. The local references are personal and mostly Scottish.

Eye to the Future.
This poem sequence of fourteen poems was written during the run-up
  to and the immediate aftermath of the 2014 Scottish independence
  referendum. Fortune's whirligigs and Time's revenges have made some
  of them appear already dated and others more relevant. However, they
  capture some of the attitudes and feelings that were widely on display
  in Scotland at the time. The concrete poem on the title-page plays
  with the words in Scots, English, Gaelic, Spanish and Catalan for "eye",
  "always", "yes", "I", "there is" and "future".
Better Thegither. "Better Together" was the slogan of the No Campaign in
  the referendum.
The Right Hon. PM Speaks. "Right" has always been David Cameron's
  favourite word.
Primary Sources. Personal memories from primary school.
Mirror Image. A popular television series, *Borgen*, brought Danish
  politics, with its interesting parallel possibilities, to Scottish attention.
Ingratitude. During the referendum campaign, the Spanish Prime
  Minister, mindful of the relevance to Catalonia, expressed hostility
  to the idea of Scottish independence. After the death of King Robert
  the Bruce, the 'Good' Sir James Douglas placed his heart in a casket
  and took it with him on crusade. In Spain he joined in a campaign
  against the Moors in Granada, and died fighting in battle, following
  Bruce as he had often done in the past. During the Spanish Civil War,
  many Scots joined the International Brigade. They are remembered
  by a statue in Glasgow of the notable Spanish Communist leader, 'La
  Pasionaria'.
The Human Chain: 11/09/13. La Diada: the Catalan National Day. At five
  o'clock in the afternoon of the 11th September, 2013, 400,000 Catalans
  joined hands to form "una cadena humana", a human chain, the length
  of Catalonia from the French border in the north to the Province of
  Valencia in the south. A further 1.6 million demonstrators for a Catalan
  Independence referendum came out on the streets of Barcelona.
Aye, Man, Aye. Despite the apparent defeat of the Yes Campaign, it
  continued to flourish and grow, until, in May of 2015, the Scottish
  National Party obtained a near total victory in the General Election in
  Scotland.
The Verdict. An image of a speculative future. The last line refers
  obliquely to the Great Tapestry of Scotland, which has been on display
  in various Scottish locations. There is a reference to W.H. Auden in the
  first sonnet section: "History to the defeated may say Alas/but cannot
  help or pardon."

Afterword

Several of the poems in *Redomones* have appeared elsewhere, in *The Herald*, *Perspectives*, *NorthWords Now*, *ScotLit* and *The Smeddum Test*. "Mirror Image" won Joint First Prize in the McCash Scots Poetry Competition 2013. "Stone Poem" is inscribed on the Standing Stone currently on display in the Cultybraggan Heritage Centre, Comrie. A few other poems first appeared in my early pamphlets, *Kindly Clouds* and *The Bountiful Loch*.

The Dedication and poems celebrating the life and achievement of R.B. Cunninghame Graham arise out of my involvement over several years in the editing of his Collected Stories and Sketches (published by Kennedy & Boyd in five volumes). At this moment in Scotland's history, a revival of interest in what he said, wrote and did during a long and productive life is a welcome development.

Finally I can only apologise for the extensive Notes section. Once a teacher ......

Alan MacGillivray

CPSIA information can be obtained
at www.ICGtesting.com
Printed in the USA
LVOW12s1633290916
506736LV00004B/965/P